WHEN CANCER SAVED MY LIFE

A heart-warming and inspirational story of a woman's journey to happiness and harmony

Millicent Pierre-Louis

WHEN CANCER SAVED MY LIFE
A heart-warming and inspirational story of a woman's
journey to happiness and harmony
Millicent Pierre-Louis

Copyright © 2015
All Rights Reserved
ISBN: 978-0-9932237-0-9

Photograph by Magnús Andersen

Book cover by Tania Cearreta

Printed in the United Kingdom

TABLE OF CONTENTS

DEDICATION

T his book is dedicated to my son, Nicholas, without
whom my life would be empty and without
meaning. The words in this poem and in the pages of this
book are dedicated to him.

A Mother's Love for Her Child

You are my child,
given to me by some miracle
that I cannot comprehend
I was worthy of.
You've come and blessed my life.

You are my world.
Whatever I've known as my own
now shared willingly
and freely with you.
You've come and opened my heart.

You are my hope,
in a world that's so unforgiving;
in your eyes I see promise
of better things yet to come.
You've come and filled me with joy.

You are my happiness
personified, yet lit even brighter
and with unimaginable beauty

created in God's light.
You've come and saved my soul.

You are my love, unconditional
whether it is given or received
and have given me complete
and utter trust in your life.
You've come and given me ambition.

For all these things
you have given me,
I have become a better soul.
For this I do promise you
my love forever,
and ever to become more like you.

Lee Degnan

INTRODUCTION

I am grateful to you for picking up this book and reading it. The most important thing I want you to know before I begin sharing the story of how cancer saved my life is this: this is not only a book about cancer. This book, this story, has been years in the making. And while, yes, cancer has played a pivotal role in it, the story I am compelled to share is one of surviving, thriving, and living your best life whether cancer is a part of that life or not.

The idea for this book was not my own, not originally. Throughout my breast cancer treatment, I was in regular sessions with a therapist by the name of Gosia Gorna at The Haven Breast Cancer Charity in London. During a routine therapy session, she casually suggested that I write a book about my experience with cancer and the profound changes it has made in my life. I thought she was crazy.

I am a mother, a cancer survivor, and a professional, but a writer I am not. In fact, I have more reasons than most to *not* be a writer. For one thing, I am slightly dyslexic, and I have hated writing for much of my life. I used to break out in a cold sweat during my English lessons at school when my English teacher asked us to write a story. I would have rather boiled my head or walked on hot coal than write.

Later in life, I worked as a secretary at the International Maritime Organisation (IMO) and was leaving my job to become a recruitment consultant. Upon receiving my resignation, my boss remarked, "I think you will make a much better recruitment consultant." He then said that I couldn't possibly be worse as a recruitment consultant than I had been as a secretary. It was harsh, but honest feedback. I was terrible at drafting letters and proposals; my boss had to constantly request I correct my errors and resubmit, and he was quite relieved to find a new secretary, someone who didn't get heart palpitations at the thought of writing. He ushered me out the door and didn't even require that I work through my two weeks' notice. So, when my therapist recommended I write this book, the idea couldn't have been further from my comfort zone and my skill set. And yet, the idea stuck.

I started a blog as part of a marketing course I took. I blogged my own story, "Overcoming Challenges with Faith," and shared how cancer saved my life. The feeling of release and freedom I felt in writing my story was profound; it was nothing I ever could have anticipated. I enjoyed sharing my story for not only the clarity it brought to me, but also for the joy it seemed to bring others. The feedback from readers was positive, and some people even commented that they found it helpful, inspiring, uplifting, and touching. Through this, the idea of writing a book sunk in a little deeper. Ultimately, writing this book became less of someone else's idea and more about something I simply had to do for myself and for others.

As I settled into the idea of writing this book, I was inundated by fears that I never anticipated. I was afraid I would have nothing to say in a book, afraid that my story wouldn't be good enough, afraid of not feeling I had a right to tell my story, and afraid that no one would be interested. I sought professional help for my newfound fears and began working through them with Life Coach Tiffany Missiha. Tiffany has helped me face my fears and my feelings of not being good enough. She helped me find the confidence I needed to write my story.

As I think back on my life before cancer and the things I've learned along the way to becoming a cancer survivor, one of the most cherished lessons I've learned is that we are all connected. To share what I have found to be true through the course of my journey is to honour the connection we have, you and I, one with another. My story, my triumphs, can be a lesson for more than me alone. So, I set aside my fear of writing to complete this book in the hope that it may inspire others to live their very best life.

This book is not meant to be a medical guide, a cancer survival plan, or an academic discourse on overcoming adversity. I do not claim to be an expert or an academic. The only credentials I have come from surviving cancer and an intention to help.

Even in that, I am by no means unique. Nearly every person on Earth either knows someone who has died from cancer, is fighting cancer, has overcome cancer, or has combated cancer themselves. But within each of these occurrences is a story of how cancer affected a life. My experience with cancer isn't unique, but how it profoundly affected my life is. Mine isn't a story of how cancer ruined my life, or ended my life, or defined my life. Rather, mine is a story of how cancer *saved* my life. I'll share that tale with you here.

My story is not meant to be taken as a recipe for survival. Rather, whether you've had cancer or not, my story is about taking any challenge life presents and learning from it, growing from it, and thriving in spite of it and because of it. We all have catalysts in our life, whether that catalyst is cancer or not. For me, cancer was my personal catalyst. For you, maybe it's a divorce, the loss of a loved one, a personal epiphany, or a sudden spark to reach for more, grow more, and gain more in your life. Whatever that catalyst is for you (and I'll be the first to say that I sincerely, truly hope it isn't cancer), I urge you to take my story as encouragement that it may be the start of great things, even when it initially feels devastating.

I hope my story helps you to realise there is always the potential for good to come out of any difficult situation. I am living proof of that and so utterly grateful that cancer saved my life. By writing the truths I've uncovered on my journey, I hope your life also will flourish and bloom. If that happens, I know my own hardship will have been for the greater good.

Chapter 1

THE EARLY YEARS

"Nobody can go back and start a new beginning, but anyone can start today and make a new ending."
[Maria Robinson]

M y story begins on the Caribbean island of Dominica, the place of my birth. It is a very small island located about halfway between the French islands of Guadeloupe and Martinique. Dominica is sometimes referred to as "Nature Island" on account of its tropical rainforests, which cover two-thirds of the island, and the beautiful and rare birds that inhabit it. It also boasts 365 rivers, one for every day of the year.

Before I was born, my parents immigrated to the United Kingdom in 1958. Like thousands of Caribbean immigrants, they hoped to find better employment opportunities and a better life there. When they arrived, things weren't quite as they expected.

The disparity between Dominica and the UK could not have been more profound. In Dominica, my parents were accustomed to sunshine and lots of it, a slower pace of life, the rural beauty and charm of island life, and the comforting feeling of belonging. In the UK, everything was different. More often than not, the weather was cold and grey. The people were different in appearance, often walking around wrapped up in dark coloured coats and with serious, focused looks on their faces. The attitudes and way of life of people in the UK was a far cry from the casual, lazily rhythmic way the islanders back home went about their daily lives. Nothing felt comfortable and warm; nothing felt like home.

The weather alone was a shock for my parents. Leaving behind balmy island heat and greeting London's fog and dampness was quite disarming. My mother said that as soon as they stepped off the boat in Tilbury, they wanted to get right back on it and return home. The dreariness they encountered didn't extend only to the weather. The people were dreary too. Remember, this was in the late 1950s, not too many years after the ending of World War II. There was still a lingering cloud of austerity and soberness that blanketed the mood of the people in London; they were rattled by the years of war, unsure of themselves, and unsure of strangers. Even their dress was dampened and dark; sturdy, serviceable clothing was the norm. My parents were accustomed to the bright, cheerful colours of Dominica, not the sooty greys of the skies and people around them.

My parents didn't feel particularly welcomed in the United Kingdom. They were on the receiving end of experiencing both skepticism towards foreigners and immigrants as a remnant of the war, and scepticism toward black people in general. The white people viewed the blacks with suspicion and were rather reluctant to rent rooms to them. As a result, my parents stuck together with other immigrants as a means of leaning on some familiarity for strength. Doing so led to them seeking accommodations in over-crowded houses. In rooms rented to them by the small minority of white landlords who didn't mind having black occupants.

It's an understatement to say their living conditions were less than ideal. The first place they lived after arriving in London was a small, terraced house with about four couples sharing two bedrooms and one bathroom. Though crowded, having a home filled with familiar faces from back home was surely a comfort to my parents. And yet, so many things were foreign to them; everything was, really. From street lights to indoor plumbing to navigating through a bustling urban metropolis, literally everything around them was a reminder of how far from home they were.

Within a few years of arriving in London, my parents got married and my mother became pregnant. Before long, they had two babies, aged one and two, with another one on the way (me). They were still sharing that small living space. I can't imagine how cramped it must have felt to share one room with their two children. The lack of privacy along with not having the space to spread out or even have the openness and spaciousness of being surrounded by land, like they had in Dominica, must have been quite depressing. Their room was not only cramped, it was also dangerous. There was a paraffin heater in the middle of the room for heat and for boiling water and washing. It was a constant safety hazard, especially with two small children.

It couldn't have been an easy decision, but like many of their friends in similar situations at the time, my parents decided that my pregnant mother would return home to Dominica with my brother and sister. My father stayed in London and worked to save up enough money for a deposit on a house. Upon returning home in 1962, my mum gave birth to me. When I was eighteen months old, she left me and my siblings in Dominica with my grandmother and returned to the United Kingdom to rejoin my father.

Although my parents weren't well-educated or skilled workers of any particular trade, they had made the decision to migrate from their home to the United Kingdom where they worked hard at low-paying jobs to build a better future for themselves and, more importantly, for their children. They set about with steely determination and scrimped and saved every penny they earned for a deposit on a house. They rented a room in a variety of small, over-crowded houses in poor working class areas in East London to keep rent expenses down so they could save more.

Once my mum left, I remember feeling a great sense of loss and abandonment. Though I was very young, I recall these feelings clearly and acutely. I missed the love and affection my mum would shower us with; I missed her smell and her warm lips against my cheeks. My grandmother reassured us that one day our parents would send for us and that we would be reunited as a family, but that didn't go very far towards dispelling my feelings of abandonment, which never left me. I remember overhearing my grandmother and great aunt speaking about when my mum would return. "Soon, I hope," my grandmother would say. "Raising these children at my age is taking its toll on me; I'm too old and tired to keep track of these children for much longer."

Of course, my grandmother did her very best to take care of us, but it was hard for her. She was in her early seventies and slowing down, and my siblings and I could exhaust the patience of a saint. We lived in the middle of the countryside on a steep hill far from the main road and close to a ravine. I remember the three of us always getting into mischief and constantly being scolded by our uncle, auntie, and grandmother. At times, it felt like the whole community, which consisted of perhaps five families, was watching out for our antics.

In our rural area, the houses were scattered among the lush green vegetation in small groups of twos and threes. We had no running water and our toilet was a small outhouse with a large wooden shelf with a round hole cut out of it. Once perched precariously on the top, you would take care of your business. There was no electricity; we lit our two-room home with candlelight and kerosene lamps. Despite all the challenges this rural life presented us with, ours was an enjoyable life filled with simple pleasures and surrounded by temperate climates, natural beauty, and a freedom we have never experienced since. I cannot imagine entertaining three children in such a setting without electricity and running water, with hardly any toys or age-appropriate activities to keep children entertained. Keeping the three of us out of trouble was a formidable challenge, one my grandmother was growing weary of.

Meanwhile, I ached to see my parents, particularly my mother. I had yet to meet my father at that point; he'd been unable to return for a visit to Dominica since my birth. As I overheard my grandmother saying how much she wished my parents would return for us, I couldn't help but agree. It was nearly five years before they were finally able to send for my sister and me. My brother had been able to move to London a year earlier to be with my parents, and I was extremely envious of him. Some family friends had taken him by boat to the UK, and though the journey took a trying two weeks during which he became seriously ill, I would have traded places with him in an instant.

At the age of five, I was told the news that I had been longing to hear: our parents were in a position to have my sister and I join them in London. I was elated. To this day I remember how happy I felt to hear that I was finally going to see my mother, meet my father for the first time, and live together with my parents and siblings as a family. I was especially excited because during the time my parents and I had been apart, my mother had given birth to another child and I was very eager to meet my baby brother for the very first time.

The day finally arrived for my sister and me to travel from our rural village in the mountains to the airport. The actual distance between our home and the airport was not very far, but due to the poor conditions of the roads and debris from landslides, it was a two-hour trek for us. The airport was on one end of the island and our home was on the other with snaking, winding roads between. Traveling along rough roads was laborious and slow-going so we had to wake very early to make the trip. However, even if it would have taken many hours more to get to the airport, I wouldn't have cared; I was so excited to finally be travelling to London to join my parents. It was a remarkable, joyous day for me.

We had a travelling companion who accompanied us from Dominica to London, and though I can't recall this detail precisely, I doubt my sister and I were much trouble for the companion. We were both wide-eyed and taking it all in, quietly anticipating the unknown ahead of us in our own way. What would London be like? What would it be like to live in a big city with our parents?

Our parents met us at London Airport where we were joyously reunited. My first impression of London was of the many lights flickering and making strange colourful shapes in the distance as the car sped past. Everything was so brightly lit, a stark contrast for a five-year-old accustomed only to sunlight, candlelight, and kerosene.

My parents borrowed a car from a friend in order to transport us from the airport. I spent a good portion of the ride staring out the window, taking in my foreign new surroundings. Unfortunately, I spent another good portion of the ride emptying my stomach all over the backseat of the borrowed car. I was unaccustomed to travelling in a car at such high speeds, something which I had never done in my short life up to that point.

I found England to be a strange country in many ways, much the same as my parents had before me. It took us quite some time to settle into our new environment where everything was so peculiar and different. We had to grow accustomed to the cold weather, which I didn't particularly care for. Everything about the food was bizarre to me, including how it was prepared. In Dominica, we had cooked our meals over small wood-fuelled fires in a small cook-house. In our new house, I was fascinated by the blue flames that flickered from a large white object in the kitchen commonly known as a cooker. I also remember thinking that no matter where I went, there were so many people. There were people everywhere, so much so that I could smell the closeness of their bodies everywhere I went. Gone was the sweet-smelling fresh air and gone was the wide open, lush, green space of our island paradise.

My parents had not wasted their time apart from us. They had worked hard and saved their money. For their efforts, they'd been able to buy a three-bedroom terraced house in a reasonably nice area with a large park just around the corner. Two of the rooms were being rented out, but it was still lovely to be together with my family in our very own home. Like many people at the time, they rented bedrooms to other immigrants to help pay their mortgage. It's strange, but life seems to have repeated itself as all these years later I am doing the exact same thing my parents did.

We were enrolled at the local primary school. My brother and sister were older so they started school first, with my enrollment following in the next term. Despite the culture shock of relocating to London, I have to say growing up in East London was a great adventure for small island children like us. We had lots of friends, most of whom lived on the same street. The local school was a five-minute walk from our home, and we would call on our friends and walk to school together as a group. School holidays were great fun, an opportunity to explore the local area and get into all sorts of mischief while our parents were at work.

My siblings and I had chores to do on a daily basis as our parents both worked long hours. As such, we were expected to contribute to the smooth running of our home. So, from the age of eleven years old, along with my sister, I had the responsibility of cooking the family meal and having it ready for the family to eat at 6pm when my parents returned home from work. Responsibility for preparing the evening meal always took priority over homework or extracurricular activities. We were latch-key children, meaning we each had a key to the front door and used it to let ourselves in after school while our parents were at work.

My mum was without a doubt the matriarch and driving force behind the family. Although she had very little schooling and never really developed a love of reading and writing, you could never pull one over on her. If there was a decision to be made regarding the children or anything relating to the home, she was always the one who made things happen and took full responsibility for the smooth running of our home.

An example of mum's presence as the matriarch happened one afternoon when we came home to witness my father having a rather heated argument with one of the male guests. It quickly turned into the two of them pushing and shoving one another in the lean-to attached to the kitchen. My mum, who was in another part of the house at the time, rushed into the kitchen when she heard the commotion to see my father being held by the scruff of his neck by the male guest who was about a foot taller. My mum rushed to my father's defense while shouting at the top of her voice at the guest to let go of my father. It seemed to make him come to his senses because he released his grip on my Father, who was clearly shocked and a little disorientated.

To say that my mum was angry with the guest would be an understatement. She gave him his marching orders, telling him to leave the house there and then. The guest, who wasn't the least bit pleased at being evicted without notice, called the police and they arrived shortly after. The police knocked on the door and my father invited then in, whereupon he began to explain to the policeman what had happened. The policeman told my father he had to give the guest two weeks' notice to vacate the property.

On hearing this, my mother, who was adamant that the man be forced to leave, stepped forward and said with tremendous resolve, "Officer, this man has just assaulted my husband and there is no way he can remain under this roof." With that, the policeman informed the guest very politely that he had to vacate the premises immediately. Under the watchful eye of the policeman, the guest gathered up all of his possessions and left the house.

As I said, mum was always the one who took charge.

My father was a very attractive, charismatic man who could charm the birds out of the trees. He spent a lot of time out of the home, either working at his job on the railways or out with his friends. I always had the impression that he was happy to leave everything to my mother. He seemed quite content to go to work, or spend time with his friends discussing politics and drinking rum or watching cricket during the summer months, rather than get involved with the day-to-day issues regarding the running of the house or raising the children.

As the years went by, my parents' relationship began to deteriorate. One thing that always stuck with me while growing up was a sense of not being a family. There seemed to be a feeling of discord, and I think this was largely due to our parents' frequent arguments, which made for a heavy atmosphere in the home. When they weren't arguing, they seemed to be complaining about us kids, whether it was a case of how noisy we were or the fact that we had just broken one of mum's ornaments or a window while we were playing cricket in the garden. We must have broken windows often because my Father at one point decided not to replace the panes of broken glass in the lean-to after we broke them playing cricket.

My father began to spend more and more time out with his friends, leaving my mum to raise us. They constantly argued and at times their arguments would escalate into violent ones. I remember quite vividly one Sunday when my parents had an enormous argument that ended in a physical fight which caused our neighbours to come banging on our front door. I don't remember what exactly the argument was about. I just remember that my father punched my mum, leaving her with a horrible black eye.

The day after was a school day by which time my mother's eye was completely swollen and bruised and half closed. She told me she wanted to visit a friend and I remember thinking she probably wanted someone to speak to about the fight. Visiting her friend meant she would walk past my school with me, and then onward to her friend's home. I was so ashamed of the black eye she had, and I didn't want anyone to see me with my mum looking like that. I guess I was worried that I would have to explain to my friends why my mum had a black eye if they saw her. So, I didn't wait for her to walk with me; instead, I made up some excuse, grabbed my school bag, and ran out the door to school leaving her staring after me.

To this day, I look back on that situation and experience waves of regret. The feeling that I was disloyal to my mum in that situation remains with me. I feel so ashamed that I didn't have the strength of character to stand up and say, "I don't care what people say! You are my mum and I'm going to be there for you and support you!" I was eleven then. I somehow feel I should have known better. All these years later, I have finally forgiven myself for my actions and the feeling of guilt which plagued me for so long. As a child, I couldn't possibly have been expected to understand the actions or the motives of an adult displaying such anger.

A few years later, my parents separated. I remember feeling a tremendous sense of relief when mum informed us she was going to divorce our dad. The decision surely weighed heavily on my mum at that time; divorce was often met by rejection and shunning by other Dominican women in the community, but she chose to divorce our dad anyway. I remember thinking then how brave and courageous my mum was, and I even viewed her as somewhat of a champion of women's rights. I was very, very proud of her.

My father was stunned by my mum's decision. He never thought for an instant that my mum had it in her to make such a decision and see it through. A few weeks after their divorce, my father decided to wait for my mum under a bridge where she crossed over to catch a bus to and from work. He disguised himself with dark glasses and a hat and waited for her to walk by. He assaulted her and had it not been for a passerby who shouted at him to let her go, her injuries may have been much worse. The case went to court and a judge punished him with two weeks in prison for breach of the injunction that prevented him from going near my mum and for the assault. After that, my father kept his distance.

For the next five years, my parents never exchanged a word. Our father completely ignored us and didn't even provide any financial assistance for our care. Needless to say, times were very hard financially. We had difficulty paying for necessities, including coal, which fuelled the central heating system. There was seldom extra to pay for holidays or days out. And yet, despite things being difficult for us, we were all very happy that there would be no more fighting, and we were grateful to be able to relax and enjoy being with each other.

There were several particularly cold days. We had no coal to light the coal boiler to start the central heating system, and we had no money to buy coal. We came home from school, grabbed one of our mum's coats, and sat at the dining room table to do our homework. We had to blow on our hands or hug a hot mug of tea to keep our fingers from becoming too numb to do our assignments.

Somehow we managed, and on occasion, we even found that having no money had its advantages. When the second-hand television broke, which it did frequently, we had no problem finding ways to entertain ourselves with games or other free family activities. We were able to get free meals at school and assistance buying our school uniforms. I don't believe we really missed what we didn't have. We were simply happy that our house wasn't full of arguing and violence. We would have traded that for being poor any day.

Throughout our time of financial hardships, my mum adamantly held onto our house. She didn't want to disrupt our childhood any further by relocating us on top of everything else we had endured. She ended up remortgaging the house and buying out my father's share. To make ends meet, she took any work she could find, including low-paying jobs in factories, hospitals, and schools. My mum was a determined, focused, and hard working woman, who always put our needs before her own.

Intentional or not, she gave me another gift as well. I grew up being very self-sufficient and tenacious. My mum wasn't an overly affectionate parent, and we worked hard to earn her praise. However, our happiness was always her number one priority, and she did everything possible to minimise the disruption in our lives. She is my hero in every sense of the word. Despite the rockiness of many situations in my childhood, I feel blessed beyond words to have grown up with a mum who did all she could for us.

Chapter 2

AS AN ADULT

"The best love is the kind that awakens the soul and makes us reach for more, that plants a fire in our hearts and brings peace to our minds. And that's what you've given me. That's what I'd hoped to give you forever."
[Nicholas Sparks]

M y adult years were no less adventurous than my childhood, if not more so. We leave behind childhood years only to find ourselves on a path through adulthood that presents us with even more opportunities to grow up. I left school at eighteen, eager to be an adult and start my *real* life. I wasn't sure what I wanted from this real life, but I was eager just the same.

One of the first jobs I took was with the Ministry of Defence as a civil servant. It took me six months to make it through the zillion interviews and mountains of paperwork that secured the position. Steady work with a reputable employer seemed worth the effort, at least initially.

After only two weeks, I surprised my family and friends, and even myself a little, by handing in my resignation. No one could understand why I would walk away from a well-paying job with an excellent pension to work for a small, unknown tour operator, but that's exactly what I did. I had the smallest doubt about my decision, but my colleagues' reaction to my resignation sealed the decision for me. I told the girls in the typing pool that I was leaving, and one of the girls piped up to ask, "But what about your non-contributory pension scheme?" After that, I couldn't leave that job fast enough. At eighteen, a pension scheme was the last thing on my mind. I wanted to think about adventure, not retirement.

At the time, in the early 1980s, packaged holidays were becoming extremely popular. There was a new tour operator in town called Tjaereborg Holidays that was headed by a feisty female managing director who wanted to shake up the travel industry by encouraging people to change the way they booked their holidays. These were exciting times for the industry, so when I was offered the opportunity to work for them and a chance to travel the world, I grabbed it with both hands. It was far more exciting to me than working in a boring job in an office with a good pension, especially when retirement seemed lifetime away. Or so I thought. In truth, for the first month I worked for the tour operator, I spent every single day, all day, stuffing flight tickets in envelopes—there was no adventure in that.

In the great tradition of the flightiness of an eighteen-year-olds' thought processes, by week four I was seriously considering approaching the Ministry of Defence and asking for my old job back, but I refrained. I made the decision to tough it out and endured my fair share of paper cuts and mundane tasks, and I'm so glad I did. Shortly after, our managing director decided to implement a company rule whereby in order to enhance our knowledge of the hotels and resorts we sold, we would need to sample the holidays ourselves. We were permitted to take four weeks of free holidays from their brochure, and we could bring along a spouse or a friend for half price! At this point, I felt that my decision to leave the Ministry made me a genius.

Yvonne, my colleague and friend, would come by my desk and ask, "So, Millie, where should we go for our holiday this quarter?" We would rub our hands together with glee and begin choosing the four and five-star hotels where we would choose to stay. These were very happy days, and I had some amazing holidays at wonderful resorts in the Mediterranean as a result.

Looking back, my time at Tjaereborg Holiday was the best time of my life. I was nineteen years old and I was given the opportunity to travel to amazing places and stay at luxurious hotels. It was a far cry from the austere and frugal environment I had grown up in. Often my mum would ask me, "Are you off again? This house is not a hotel; all you seem to do is come home, change your clothes, pack your bags, and then you're off again!" I never paid too much attention to her nagging as I knew this was an opportunity of a lifetime, and one I had no intention of passing up.

I spent many a day languishing on a beautiful sunny beach and enjoying the sumptuous luxury of the hotel nightclubs in the evening, gyrating to the beat of disco music. I was having the time of my life, and I felt as free as a bird. It was wonderful.

On one particular occasion, I stayed at a very luxurious hotel on the Canary Island of Lanzarote. I was nineteen, and it was the very first time I went abroad on my own. I treated myself to a sauna at the hotel. Unbeknown to me, the sauna was mixed. Thus, I walked into the sauna, where I was greeted by two naked, very large, and well-endowed gentlemen seated on a bench casually chatting to one another. Well, I closed the door so quickly that I stubbed my toe on the door whilst struggling to hide my embarrassment and shock. Besides that, I had many wonderful experiences and saw some amazing sights. I met wonderful people, some of whom I am still in touch with some thirty-five years later. These amazing experiences shaped me into the person I am today, and I wouldn't trade them for the world.

After about twelve years, I left the travel industry and worked in various other industries until I was offered a position as a recruitment consultant. I quickly found that I loved meeting people and placing them in jobs that would be rewarding and fulfilling to them, as well as to their employers. It could be quite challenging, but it proved to be financially rewarding and professionally satisfying as well.

The years rolled by quickly, and before I knew it, I was forty-four years old. I was single and for the first time ever, I started to panic a little. I found myself scared to death of being left on the shelf. I began to have flashes of myself as an old spinster sitting in my chair knitting with a cat on my lap, having just enjoyed a microwave meal for one. Although there is nothing wrong with such a scene, it wasn't how I had envisioned my twilight years. On top of that, I was desperate to become a mother. With my professional life trucking along steadily, the pull to be in a relationship and have a child was undeniably strong. Unfortunately for me, I had experienced some health issues affecting my reproductive organs, such as endometriosis, uterine fibroids, and cysts. Given these issues, coupled with my age, I knew the odds of becoming a mother were firmly stacked against me. Not to mention the fact that I was single, and there did not seem to be anyone looming on the horizon for me, at least no one I wanted to have a child with.

The good news was that I am my mother's daughter. That same fiery determination that brought her to the UK and kept her moving forward alone while raising four kids, was alive and well in me. Despite the door into motherhood seeming to be shut in front of me, I felt that until it was bolted tight and immovable, I still had a chance. I hung on to any and every shred of hope there was and considered my dream of being a mother still within reach.

So, I formulated a plan.

I was in the middle of looking for a new job, so I made the decision that I would find one that would allow me to work four days a week, Monday through Thursday. On Fridays, I would put all my efforts into looking for a husband and a suitable father for my child. It strikes me as humorous now, to think of myself plotting and scheming to find love and a parenting partner with the same level of commitment and organisation that I would put into finding a new flat or shopping for groceries. But I was determined, and that's what determination looks like sometimes.

I learned that an ex-colleague had been made managing director of a small, boutique recruitment agency in London, and I contacted her right away. I was very thankful when she was kind enough to offer me a position in the company's city office on a four day per week basis. My plan was coming together nicely. Now, I just needed to figure out where to spend my Fridays looking for a husband and a father for my child.

I signed up on as many online dating sites as I could afford and set about meeting and interviewing prospective suitors. Monday to Thursday, I interviewed prospective candidates for jobs as a recruiter; Fridays, I interviewed prospective husbands/fathers. It was great fun and my plan was coming along brilliantly. The girls in the office looked forward to my amusing tales of disastrous dates; they even suggested that I write a funny book on my dating experiences with men of all shapes, colours, and sizes (who knows, maybe I will).

After countless dates, I developed a strong case of what I like to call *date weariness*. I began to lose hope that I would find someone suitable, let alone someone I could develop strong feelings for. Then, on one very hot summer day in July 2006, I happened to be in a chat room on the internet talking to a number of men all at the same time (the search seemed more efficient this way). The chat room sites weren't nearly as sophisticated then as they are today and being rather slow at typing and rubbish at spelling, the men I was chatting with fell by the wayside, one by one. I was probably taking too long to reply to their messages and they got bored, or they were talking to so many other women who were far wittier and whose messages didn't take ages to come through.

On this day, however, there was one guy who didn't seem to care about my poor spelling and he hung in there. It may have been because he was German and English was his second language. We chatted online for a while and then he asked for my number, which I was very happy to give to him. I thought, *Why not? What do I have to lose?* It was only a phone call.

After about an hour on the phone, we agreed to meet at a quaint, old English pub near Leicester Square tube station for a few drinks. After some general chatting and sizing each other up in person, I excused myself and slipped off to the ladies' room. When I finally rejoined him at the bar, he looked at me quizzically as though to say, "I thought you'd stood me up; you were gone so long!" Little did he know I had used my time in the ladies room to call my sister and give her a detailed account of our date so far. I also thought he was gorgeous and incredibly sexy, but there was no way I was going to let him know this so early on. So for the time being, I was planning to play it cool. As the relationship developed, I felt a passion for him that I had never experienced before for anybody. I kept asking myself, *Could this gorgeous guy really fancy me?* He came across as worldly, intelligent, and every bit the gentleman. I thought I had died and gone to heaven every time I looked into his eyes. From the time of our second date, which we spent at the Air Show in Farnborough, we were inseparable. By February of the following year, we had moved in together.

The first few years of our relationship were great. We travelled a lot: Australia, Dubai, Abu Dhabi, Italy, Austria, and spent many lovely weekends at his house with his children in northern Germany. Although he had two daughters by his first wife, he was happy for us to try to have a child together, which filled me with great joy. His two girls are lovely children, and they accepted me without any problems. I thought at the time, *Finally I have found the family I always wanted!* Little did I know what fate had in store for us.

I knew having a child was not going to be easy for us, and I didn't even know if it was possible, but I was desperate to try. A few years prior to meeting this man, I had seen a consultant who specialised in fertility. The consultant had informed me that my existing medical conditions would impact my ability to conceive and he more or less implied that I stood a better chance of winning the Lottery than I did of having a child. I was devastated by this news, but at the same time I felt a strong determination to prove him wrong. So, as we began looking at our options to conceive, I ended up doing some research and found an Italian consultant gynaecologist by the name of Luciano Nardo. He specialised in reproductive medicine and surgery. We made an appointment to see him.

I felt a tremendous sense of hope during our first consultation with Mr. Nardo, who was very empathetic and willing to help us. I asked him, "What do you think the chances are of us conceiving?" He replied, "Your chances are very slim; however, anything is possible." Just hearing that phrase "anything is possible," filled me with such hope. I clung to that hope with all the desperation of a drowning woman clinging to a life vest.

Our next step was to undergo some exploratory and corrective procedures to prepare me physically to start the IVF treatment. After we began treatment, we had a number of failed attempts, and our funds began to diminish very quickly. We had enough money for only one more attempt. In the meantime, I researched a clinic in Barcelona, Spain, called the Institute Marques. I learned this clinic had a great success rate with IVF treatments, and their fees were considerably less expensive than those in the UK so we made the decision to seek their help and a few months after making the initial inquiry with the clinic in Spain, we became patients under their care. Dr. Nardo agreed to be our consultant in the UK where he would work in tandem with the team in Spain.

I felt very happy with this decision and everything seemed to be going our way. Even our travel to Spain was being paid for by my company, unbeknown to them, of course! As a recruitment consultant, the company I worked for incentivised us to meet and exceed our monthly/quarterly targets, and it just so happened that I won the incentive on two successive occasions. My gift was weekend breaks including airfare and accommodations. Needless to say, we chose to take our break in Barcelona.

We paid for our treatment in cash as this meant we would receive a substantial discount. I found myself transporting over ten thousand pounds in cash in a weekend bag through customs to Barcelona, all the while praying the money wouldn't be discovered and that I wouldn't be asked to explain why I was transporting such a large sum into another country. I had never been so nervous in my life.

Just as everything appeared to be going swimmingly, I discovered a lump on my right breast. The IVF treatment was immediately stopped. The lump was removed, and I waited in agony for a week for the test results to come back. Thankfully, the lump was found to be non-malignant. However, while I waited for the outcome of the procedure, I felt totally numb and paralysed with fear because I knew that if the lump was malignant, I would not be able to proceed with IVF treatment, now or in the future.

When we resumed the IVF treatment, after negotiating a few more hurdles, I eventually became pregnant with twins. We were overjoyed. Our joy, however, was bitter sweet when eight weeks into the pregnancy we learned that we had lost one of the babies. Still, we had kept one feotus and were so thankful for that. I could never properly describe the total joy and elation I felt when in 2010 at the age of forty-eight, I gave birth to our son, Nicholas.

After the initial joy and excitement I felt of being a new mum, the relationship between my partner and I began to unravel. The IVF treatment put a lot of strain on our relationship. I was so focused on my dream of becoming a mother that I neglected our relationship. We grew apart, we started arguing, and both of us felt misunderstood and disconnected with one another. He began to feel more and more isolated, particularly because at that time he was living in Germany and coming home only monthly. Finally, in the summer of 2011, our relationship ended. Despite the ending, I will never be able to thank him enough for the amazing gift he has given me. The most precious gift one human being can give to another: the gift of life. I truly hope he experiences the same inexhaustible joy our son gives me every day.

Chapter 3

YOU ARE STRONGER
THAN YOU THINK

"Promise me you'll always remember:
You're braver than you believe, and stronger than you
seem, and smarter than you think."
[A.A. Milne]

I was diagnosed with breast cancer in August of 2012. I had just set up my own recruitment business three months prior and in order to do so, I had given up a very well-paying job as a recruitment consultant. It was a job I absolutely loved and was very good at. I had discovered the lump in February of that year, but I had been so busy with life that I totally ignored it. I had taken a year-long maternity leave when my son was born and had only just returned to work in January of 2012. While on maternity leave, I made the decision to start my own recruitment business from home, so I took the opportunity to build an office in my garden during that time. I couldn't face the commute to the city office anymore, so I handed in my notice upon my return in January and began working from home. It was an extremely scary experience, being a single mum with a one-year-old son and having little to no contact with my son's father and very little support. Being a single mum is a challenge all of its own, and I don't know of too many things scarier than that.

My neighbour kept on at me to go to my doctor. Eventually, I gave in and made an appointment. If I had to be totally honest, I would say that I always had the feeling in the back of my mind that the lump I'd found in February was going to turn out to be something serious, but I did everything I could to suppress those thoughts. Life with Nicholas was too happy then, and I simply wasn't in the mood to let some grey clouds or threats of rain ruin it. I hoped that if I ignored the nagging at the back of my mind, perhaps the whole thing would simply go away. It didn't.

I saw my doctor in August. He quickly referred me to the local hospital and from there, things progressed quite rapidly. Three days after my initial appointment with my general practitioner, I had a visit with a consultant at the hospital, a man who was very nice but lacking in bedside manner. He was so direct, so brisk! At my first appointment with this consultant, I casually asked what he thought the lump might be. I thought this was a natural, normal question. He responded in the most direct way, and said it may be breast cancer and that he wanted me to undergo some tests to confirm his suspicions.

I don't know if I expected a little more candy-coating of his suspicions or if I had just done a really good job of talking myself out of the possibility that the lump could amount to anything serious, but his words hit me pretty hard. And yet, after reeling for a moment, I told myself that until I had the final test results, no one including this consultant could be sure it was breast cancer. I pushed any worry out of my mind and decided I wouldn't let it bother me again. I would simply wait for the test results. I left the hospital and went back to my life which, at that time, was very busy with my new business and the day-to-day duties of looking after my son.

A week later, I returned for another appointment, alone. My test results were back. Again with the direct, brisk demeanour, the consultant shared the news that it was as he suspected: I had breast cancer. My reaction was to say, "Okay, well if that's the case, what's the prognosis? And what is the treatment?" From the outset of this new hurdle in my life, I was determined to overcome it. He told me that he felt that my right breast needed to be removed as soon as possible.

As the consultant retrieved his diary and we began looking for dates when I could have a mastectomy, it felt almost as if I was observing someone else have this conversation with a consultant, and I was just an observer. I wonder now, looking back, how deeply the news of my diagnosis had sunk in at the time.

He picked a date and checked to see if it would be convenient. I responded that, yes, the date would be fine. By getting down to the business of planning and scheduling something, even something as significant as a mastectomy, I had put myself back in the driver's seat and felt in control again. However, the reality of my diagnosis began to sink in and with it, I began to realise the seriousness of the situation and its possible implications. I made a phone call to a very good friend and explained to him what had just happened, and then I made my way to the hospital chapel, where I completely broke down and sobbed my heart out. I knew that in order for me to get through this, I had to be strong, so I began to plead with God to give me the strength to overcome this illness.

For anyone who has received a cancer diagnosis, or any news that touches on the fragility of life, the emotional response I had was probably something you're very familiar with. I was scared. No, I was more than scared, I was petrified. I was scared more for my son Nicholas than I was for myself. What would happen to him if something happened to me? Who would be responsible for him? Who would raise him? The mere thought that there was even a slight possibility that I wouldn't be there to see him grow up filled me with such fear and dread. I sobbed my heart out in that chapel.

Yet, in my deep despair, I felt that I wasn't completely alone. As I knelt there by myself in the chapel, I had an overwhelming sense that I *wasn't alone,* and that through it all, even with all of this dreadful news, I was being cared for. I felt lifted up, buoyed somehow, and feeling as though God was with me giving me the strength to cope. With that realisation, peace began to sweep in and fear began to lessen its grip on me. I knew in my heart that if anyone or anything could give me the strength and courage to cope, it would be my faith and my love for my son. I simply had to come through this for my son. We had gone through so much with IVF to have Nicholas; it had been a long, emotional, and stressful process. I simply refused to believe that God would bring me through all of that, unite me with Nicholas in such a trying way, only to then separate us so early in his life. Nicholas needed me. I felt mothering Nicholas and raising him to be the best person he could be was my job and my purpose for living. I knew in my heart that I would see it through.

It's an interesting phenomenon how we deal with obstacles in our life. From the time we approach an obstacle until the time we are on the other side of it, we incrementally move from feeling as though we have no strength at all to realising we are so much stronger than we ever imagined. The switch happens so suddenly, and it would be difficult to know precisely where one ends and the other begins.

In the beginning, as was the case when I first learned of my diagnosis, we feel detached from our obstacle, denying it even exists. Then, with the realisation that it is a very real obstacle, despite the fact that we don't really want to believe it, our emotions come and we break down, we sob, we wonder how we're going to get through it, and we wonder if we'll be strong enough. Then we are reminded of all the things we have to live for and suddenly, in that instant, having the strength to overcome an obstacle becomes less a question of whether we have it or not but more a statement of determination that, yes, we *are* strong enough. It's no longer about *can* I survive; instead we are *committed* to surviving. We aren't going to merely survive; we're already plotting how we will thrive in spite of our obstacle and how we're going to minimise the impact of that obstacle on those we love.

I can't say how long this process will take for anyone else, but for me it happened very quickly. In a very short period of time, I was already thinking of ways to ensure that my current obstacle, breast cancer, didn't impact my family, especially Nicholas, more than it had to.

The news of my cancer was received differently by each member of my family. It was, of course, an initial shock for each of them, especially since my brothers and sister had always viewed me as the "healthy one" in the family. They saw me as someone who paid attention to health and what I ate and knew I had made openness to alternative therapy a part of my life. They were also well aware of the emotional and psychological stress I was already under because of a combination of some major events in the recent years of my life, such as IVF treatment, a new business start-up, and, perhaps more importantly, the breakdown of my relationship with Nicholas' father. After the initial shock passed, we agreed not to tell my elderly mum the news. She was living in Dominica at the time, and we felt the worry and stress would be too much for her, given her age and distance.

My brother, whom I didn't see much before my illness though he only lived a few miles from my home, began coming to visit me weekly after my diagnosis. He even pitched in to clean my house, which was much appreciated. To this day, my brother comes twice a week to clean my house. My sister, a nurse and midwife, reacted to my diagnosis by strongly encouraging me to do exactly as the doctors and consultants advised. When I diverged from the doctors' advice and investigated other means for treating my cancer, my sister was very disappointed. Though she didn't want to upset me by sharing her disappointment with me, it has unfortunately caused a rift between us, something we are working very hard to mend even to this day.

After my mastectomy and the mandatory twenty-four hours in the hospital, I was so ready to be reunited with Nicholas that I simply refused to stay in the hospital any longer. With my surgeon's consent to discharge me, and my handbag slung over my shoulder, I left the hospital with my sister and was on the local bus making my way home the very next day. I was so desperate to see my son, so desperate to minimise the impact of my illness on Nicholas' life.

Through the course of my cancer diagnosis, and the treatment and operation that followed, my son was the primary reason I went looking for strength in a way I never had before. Along the way, I learned quite a bit more about strength in truly amazing fashion. During this time, I had to dig deep to find the strength and courage to overcome the despair I was experiencing, and I knew the only way I could find it was to ask God for help. I felt that my prayers were heard and that through God, I was able to call on a strength that I never knew existed. I believe God gave me the courage and the strength to not only overcome my situation, but to grow as a result of my experiences.

Strength through Knowledge

There are many different forms of breast cancer. I was diagnosed with infiltrating ductual carcinoma of the right breast. The doctors felt the best treatment would be a mastectomy followed by five rounds of chemotherapy. Between the time I was diagnosed in August and the time of my mastectomy in October of the same year, I found strength in knowledge. Even the decision to have a mastectomy wasn't a rushed one and I took a great deal of time to investigate and research treatment options on my own. Of course, it is very important for anyone with a cancer diagnosis to choose treatment options in collaboration with medical professionals, but there is an added measure of strength that comes when we take an active role in discovering what options exist. Yes, our life is in the hands of the professionals, but we also have a responsibility to ourselves to know our options.

After I was diagnosed, I researched online, bought books, and sought the advice of alternative therapists, all while listening to my body. I learned that there is a tremendous amount of information out there, and I felt it was very important for me to look into the more reputable sources so I could make informed decisions about my treatment plan. I found tremendous strength in this approach.

Before I agreed to a mastectomy, I researched and found a doctor in Rome who offered alternative treatments for cancer. I emailed him and he agreed to give me an appointment. Shortly after, a friend and I booked a flight to Rome to meet him. After a consultation with this doctor, I ultimately decided the therapy he offered really wasn't for me, so I declined becoming a patient of his. However, I didn't consider this a loss. As I said, there is strength in acquiring knowledge and making informed decisions about your own body. I also looked at a number of other alternative therapies and employed the services of a dietician. She prepared me extremely well for my treatment and recovery with information on nutritional supplements and food preparation, which ultimately led to a much quicker recovery.

On account of the time I spent researching and investigating, by the time I scheduled my mastectomy and began chemotherapy I was much stronger mentally than when I first started my cancer journey. A lot of the fear was gone, replaced by a strength I had gained through educating myself on my options.

Believe in Your Strength

Every one of us has an inner strength that we're likely unaware of until we need it the most. When we have a troubling experience in our lives or a tragedy takes place, often times our initial reactions are those of denial, fear, and uncertainty. Through my own experience, I've learned to recognise and deal with these types of reactions with a more positive frame of mind. Look for something you believe in *outside of yourself*, a force that is greater than you. This is not only absolutely essential to surviving any tragedy, but it is also a source of amazing strength. It gives you the courage to embrace a strength you never knew you had within you.

For me, that source of strength came from God. For you, it may be a completely different set of circumstances and a completely different source. The point is not in the particulars; it's in recognising that we all have obstacles presented to us and that these obstacles can each be overcome by letting go of our knee-jerk, fearful reactions and by actively seeking a source of strength to guide us.

As I continued pulling on the strength I found deep down inside, supported by my faith in God, I found myself praying an awful lot. After returning from my trip to Rome and realising that the alternative therapy offered by Dr. Simoncini was not right for me, I was initially quite discouraged. It seemed I was running out of options for avoiding a mastectomy, and this was emotionally difficult for me to deal with. Then, some other friends and I went to Portugal to see the Shrine of Our Lady of Fatima. I drew a lot of inner strength and courage from that experience and when I returned home, I felt strong enough to make the decision that I would move forward with a mastectomy. I felt peaceful and even happy with the decision.

Having inner strength from my faith and from the support of my family and friends meant that I wasn't consumed by fear. I wasn't bitter, and I didn't feel like a victim. Rather, I felt strong and empowered to make the decisions that were right for me in order to overcome the obstacle of breast cancer.

Find Support for Your Strength

I began to wonder whether the inner strength I was finding was something I was developing through sheer will power. Or, was it always there lying dormant for a time like this? I wondered if it was something I had to practice accessing or if it would develop all on its own. I have found that the answer to these questions resides in whether or not we put ourselves in an environment where strength has the opportunity to flourish and pulse through us. To explain how I arrived at this, let me tell you what I observed.

When I wasn't surrounding myself with positive people and positive thoughts and attitudes, I had a really hard time drumming up the strength from deep within that I needed to rely on. When I consistently worked to develop a positive attitude in all areas of my life, one thought at a time, and eliminated negative emotions, such as jealousy, resentment, greed, and selfishness, the inner strength I needed was much more accessible.

Most of us spend so much time rushing around, barely making time for ourselves, our families, and our friends. One of the best ways I have found to bolster positivity in all aspects of life is to stop rushing around all the time. I have learned to take time daily to meditate, sit quietly, pray, be alone with your thoughts, and above all, appreciate the simple things in life. Though I have always been a fairly positive person, I learned to enhance my positive outlook as it became obvious that my inner strength was relying on it. During the time of my cancer treatment, I began reading books with very positive messages, such as *Courage and Confidence*, edited by Norman Vincent Peal; *Feel the Fear but Do It Anyway*, by Susan Jeffers; *You Can Heal Your Life*, by Louise Hay; and various other self-help books. I listened to videos, attended seminar workshops, and surrounded myself with positive people radiating positive energy.

Another way I retained a positive outlook was by trying to see the world and my life from a broader perspective. Many times we are so consumed by our everyday lives and the nitty-gritty details of existing that we actually become detached from the bigger picture. Our view of the world shrinks and our thoughts become focused on the smallness of our own existence. We end up burying our heads in our own problems, issues, feelings, failings, and shortcomings. We don't stop to raise our head above the parapet long enough to see that things aren't always as bad as they seem. By taking a step back, we can actually begin to put our situations into their proper perspective. By seeing things as they are, and not as they have come to feel in our small-mindedness, a positive outlook returns. When positivity returns, our inner strength begins to glow and pulse once again.

Look for the Bright Spot

If we look close enough (and sometimes we have to look *really close!*), there is a bright spot to be found in every dire situation. One of the bright spots I began to recognise was something I never could have anticipated, but it was beautiful all the same. I had a mastectomy, as I've said, and learned that as well as reconstructing that breast, they would also reconstruct the remaining breast. I had breastfed Nicholas for six months and honestly, it felt like that remaining breast was sagging right down to my knees as a result! Because of the augmentation, I now have the breast of a twenty-five-year old!

Because of all I have been through, I have been given tremendous confidence as a mother and as a woman. This confidence came from realising how much strength, gentleness, and compassion I have found through my experience. Because of this new confidence, I decided not to have a nipple reconstruction for the simple reason that I do not wish to waste any more of my precious time undergoing further surgery. I now realise that the sum total of who I am was never determined by my body, finances, or social standing. I know I will meet the person

I will have an amazing relationship with and that they will be a great father to my son and accept me for who I am, regardless of the fact that I have one breast smaller than the other, minus a nipple! This knowledge is extremely liberating, and I have never felt better about myself and my femininity. What a blessing!

After a two-year journey with cancer, having gone through the highs and the lows, I am now in a position where I am happy. I can appreciate the lessons this illness has taught me. If we have faith and dig deep within ourselves, we can triumph over any obstacle. I feel that I am a completely different person now compared to who I was before I was diagnosed. I have a greater appreciation of life, family, and friends, and I have managed to combat many fears and insecurities. Rather than seeing cancer as a terrible thing that happened *to me*, I can truly say that being diagnosed with breast cancer ultimately gave me so much more than it took away.

Each of us has obstacles we wish we could overcome. Whether that obstacle is called cancer or not, I want you to know that there is hope for overcoming it. The strength I found in battling cancer is the same strength that can be found inside you. It is there and, as I learned, we are stronger than we think we are. By finding the reasons to draw on your inner strength, like living for my son was for me, by pulling on a higher power to help us dig deep to find that inner strength, and by surrounding ourselves with positivity and making finding knowledge a source of power and strength, you can prevail in overcoming any obstacle.

Chapter 4

BEING COURAGEOUS AND TAKING RESPONSIBILITY

"Though much is taken, much abides; and though
We are not now that strength which in old days
Moved earth and heaven, that which we are, we are;
One equal temper of heroic hearts,
Made weak by time and fate, but strong in will
To strive, to seek, to find, and not to yield."
[Alfred Tennyson]

W hen it rains, it pours. We are met with one blow, only to find there are several more to follow. It is in these times that our courage is put to the test, and we have a choice to make. Will we take the role of a victim? Or will we dig deep and do the hard thing; will we take responsibility for our life and find the strength to do what we must?

For me, my cancer diagnosis was a dividing line of sorts. With it came an onslaught of additional challenges, decisions to be made, and financial and practical circumstances to navigate. Those were trying days filled with ample opportunity to choose between being a victim of my life and taking responsibility for my life. At the centre, my physical care and treatment stripped my life down to the bare essentials and left me with no time or energy to concern myself with anything but what was most important. As is the case with everything in my life now, I am grateful for the opportunity I had in that situation to be able to separate the important from the trivial.

The impact of my illness was tremendous on my son, although I had vowed to do all I could to prevent this, and although he was only two years old at the time. I remember quite vividly returning home after the mastectomy and being so very conscious of having been away from him, even for only one night. I was concerned about how he would take being separated from me because it was the first time we had ever been apart.

He was lying on his back and I was changing his nappy. I had just finished having a shower and had a robe on while I was changing him. He reached for the bottom of my robe and tried to open my robe and said, "Mummy, breast, breast gone!" I could not believe that he had such an understanding of what had occurred, of what had just happened to me. I was completely taken aback by what he said. At that point, I realised that I really couldn't shield him completely from what was taking place. Yet, how do you explain to a two-year-old that you have a disease that means you've got to lose your breast? It was really difficult for me to know how to proceed.

Since the mastectomy and breast reconstruction, I have spoken to him about how he felt at the time. Now that he's a bit older, he has been able to explain that he was very frightened and that he mostly was afraid that something would happen to me. In a way, realising how much he understood of my illness prompted me to find the nerve to take responsibility for what was happening in my life. Knowing that there were the small eyes of a dear boy watching me, quietly observing how I conducted myself while fighting fears of his own instilled a measure of courage in me.

I had many thoughts about Nicholas and about what would happen to him if something happened to me. Though I was undergoing chemotherapy at the time, the seriousness of my diagnosis was still a very real threat to our lives. I recalled then how desperately I had wanted to be a mother. My desire to be a mother really had gone hand-in-hand with a desire and longing to have a family of my own. Given the type of marriage and family my parents had, I desperately wanted a family that was stronger—one that wouldn't be torn apart by friction, arguments, divorce, and separation. In a very deep way, I was driven to be a mother and a good wife. In some strange way, I felt that if I could have a good and loving marriage, it would atone for the failures of my parents' marriage. So, when Nicholas' father and I separated before my cancer diagnosis, it was a bitter blow and I felt very let down and disappointed. Then, as a single mum of the child I had wanted so very much, it was yet another bitter blow to realise that the dream of a happy marriage had gone by the wayside, and the dream of a happy life as a mother was also in jeopardy. I sought counselling then, not only to help me deal with my cancer diagnosis, but to help me heal from the broken heart that had come with watching my dreams slip through my fingers.

As if dealing with heartbreak wasn't hard enough, my cancer treatment was weakening me and challenging me physically. I had the first round of chemotherapy and was scheduled in two days' time for the second of five rounds. The first round depleted my white blood cell count so thoroughly that the hospital told me I would have to delay the second round until my white blood cells had time to regenerate. My immune system was so diminished that I was told to avoid public transport and other highly populated areas for fear of becoming ill with an infection my body was too weak to fight off. I was able to receive some help from my dietitian to strengthen myself nutritionally, and over time I was able to rebuild my white blood cell count again. I experienced complete paralysis of my right arm and couldn't move it for almost a week. Terrible mouth ulcers prevented me from eating for a few days as well. So, there were quite a few physical challenges as a result of chemotherapy.

Whatever money I had before my cancer, I had put into setting up my business. I entered my cancer treatment in a very bad place financially. I had debts to pay and no income to meet those obligations. While in treatment, I received money from the Department for Works and Pensions due to my inability to work during chemotherapy treatment. Furthermore, I had decided the only way I could afford to stay in my house was to take in paying guests, just as my parents had done. I arranged for the rooms to be decorated, and my son and I moved our bedroom downstairs and shared the lounge. Initially, we slept on a mattress on the floor and guests began moving in shortly after from all over the world. We hosted guests from every continent: America, Canada, China, South Africa, India, Russia, Europe, Australia, and New Zealand.

As an aside, inviting guests into our home out of necessity turned out to be a wonderful experience, especially for my son. It gave him the opportunity to interact with people from all over the world. He has an inquisitive mind and is fascinated by people, loves to travel, and enjoys the world for the diverse, exciting, interesting place that it is. Having people live with us was a tremendous educational experience for him, and I saw it turn him into a person who is tolerant and values people of all backgrounds and cultures.

As I struggled to overcome cancer and raise my child, all with a houseful of guests, I was horrified when I received a notice that the Department for Works and Pensions expected repayment of a sum of around three thousand pounds! I was told I wasn't entitled to assistance from the Department for Works and Pensions because I had guests staying in my home. I couldn't believe it. I remember thinking, "I'll beat cancer, but these people really are trying to kill me!" Apparently someone had contacted them and informed them that I had paying guests in my home. I was beginning to believe in a conspiracy theory by that point.

After some toing and froing, they passed my case to their debt collections department, which then sent me a few ridiculous letters asking me to pay three thousand pounds within a month. I thought perhaps the chemotherapy had affected my brain, because I just couldn't believe how crazy the whole situation was.

I know what doesn't kill you makes you stronger, but at that point, I got on my knees and started to pray. I wondered how much more the Lord was planning on challenging me with before things started going my way. Up to that point in my life, I had always felt in control of my circumstances. But the piling on of health challenges, parenting responsibilities, financial obligations, and the addition of having debt collectors on my tail really brought my feeling of control into question. I knelt down and told the Lord I needed His help; I told Him I could no longer deal with my circumstances on my own. "Please, Lord," I said, on my knees. "Take this burden from my shoulders!" I felt inner peace sweep through me then.

I threw myself upon the mercy of the Department for Works and Pensions and explained my situation to them. I begged them to reconsider their decision to require repayment of their financial assistance to me while I was unable to work. I started writing copious amounts of letters to them, explaining and re-explaining my situation. Eventually, after a lot of back and forth, letters, and phone calls, they reviewed their earlier decision and reversed it. I'm sure you can imagine the tremendous relief I felt.

Throughout chemo, my financial woes, and the concern for my son, a concept began dawning on me which my situation forced me to explore further. I began thinking about courage and responsibility. At what point in our lives must we choose to courageously take responsibility for our lives and stop feeling like a victim of our circumstances?

Oprah Winfrey has a very good quote relating to the importance of taking responsibility for one's life. She said, "We are responsible for our own life—no other person is or ever can be." We must never forget to take responsibility; we must never divest or devolve our responsibility to other people, whether it be our partners, our parents, our children, our colleagues, or anyone else in our life.

As I considered my responsibility for my life, I realised that often times we are very willing to give other people the responsibility to make decisions that really should be ours, and we do so out of fear. We are scared and fear mishandling our responsibility, so we give that responsibility to another person. Through my circumstances, I learned that life is too short and too precious to entrust its care into the hands of anyone other than myself.

I made a conscious decision when I was diagnosed with cancer that I would take responsibility for my treatment. Yes, I placed myself *in the care of* qualified, experienced medical professionals, but I was the ultimate decision maker in my treatment plan. I researched in order to make myself well-equipped to handle the responsibility of my treatment. I received great help from two books in particular: *Chemotherapy Heals Cancer and the World is Flat* by Lothar Hirneise and *Mom's Not Having Chemo* by Laura Bond. I recommend these to anyone going through a similar struggle.

After having read these books along with additional research, combined with my dangerously low white blood count after the first of five planned chemotherapy sessions, I decided not to have any more chemotherapy. Chemotherapy simply wasn't right for me. I decided instead to pursue alternative therapies. Through the help of a dietician, Hazel Preeze, I began rebuilding my white blood cell counts. I also enlisted the help of a kinesiologist, Margaret Barclay, who was absolutely amazing and proved to be extremely beneficial in helping me to minimise the side effects of chemotherapy.

I have to stress here that the decision to use chemotherapy or not is something that will vary with each individual. With the help and advice of a medical team and loved ones, every person battling cancer must decide for themselves whether chemotherapy is right for them or not. I am in no way advocating or encouraging people to do what I did. Rather, the point is that I felt chemotherapy wasn't right for me, *and I took responsibility for that decision.* I didn't abdicate my decision related to my treatment to any other person.

I could have quite easily sat back and followed along with everything my doctors told me to do. Had I done that, knowing intuitively that chemotherapy wasn't right for me and was doing more harm than good, I don't know if I would be here today. I simply didn't react well to chemo, so I took responsibility for that and did my research. I used the information I learned to make a decision that felt right for me.

It was a scary decision to make, especially with the risks being as high as they were. That's where courage came in; it takes courage to take responsibility, but it's worth it. One of the biggest benefits is that you can't blame anybody for the outcome of your decisions. Whatever happens, you have only yourself to blame. Some may feel that's a rather intimidating responsibility, and I can understand that feeling. But here's the thing: when you take responsibility, you earn the tremendous sense of empowerment that comes with it. There is no empowerment in abdicating our decisions and responsibilities. Empowerment only comes when we choose to be responsible for our own decisions.

Knowing that you have the power to take responsibility can give you a level of confidence that is impossible to achieve if those responsibilities are delegated to others. I felt confident that I was strong enough to take responsibility, which likely played just as much of a role in my healing as the therapies I chose.

My faith was certainly tested as I stepped onto the path of taking responsibility. However, with each decision I made, my courage grew, and my faith grew. At the end of each day, I began to feel peace in knowing that whatever happened that day and every day to come, resulted in my decisions and choices. There was also peace in knowing that I would have no one to blame or be resentful towards or angry with because, ultimately, I was responsible for every single outcome.

It is my sincere hope that we all learn the power of taking responsibility for ourselves. I can't help but think what a different, better world this would be if we took responsibility for every area of our lives. Those who walk this life carrying the most resentment, which often manifests itself as negative emotions and negative consequences, are those who haven't yet discovered that they were created with all the courage they will ever need to take responsibility for themselves, their lives, and their actions. There can be no resentment towards others when the only person we can ever blame for anything is ourselves. I am so grateful for the circumstances of my life that have shown me this lifesaving, game-changing truth.

Chapter 5

YOU'RE NOT ALONE, LOVE IS ALL AROUND: OPEN UP TO LOVE

*"When tears come, I breathe deeply and rest.
I know I am swimming in a hallowed stream where many
have gone before. I am not alone, crazy, or having a
nervous breakdown … My heart is at work, my soul is
awake."* [Mary Margaret Funk]

I t's a strange phenomenon when, surrounded by family and neighbours and even guests living in your home, you come to realise that you are not alone. As silly as it might seem to have ever thought yourself alone surrounded by so many people, you are equally relieved that you now know you aren't alone. This is exactly what happened to me, and it has been one of the most important lessons I learned from my cancer experience.

Let Love Flow

Often times, we rush around. We are so cocooned in our own little world busy trying to get somewhere that we forget what really makes life worthwhile. For me, what makes life worthwhile is not what I have, who I am or what I do, but the love I give and the love I receive. My situation allowed me to focus on what is most important by taking my concentration and energy away from what wasn't. It opened my heart and my life so that love could flow in and out.

It is so important to give people the opportunity to feel good about themselves by accepting their help, support, and love, particularly at the most challenging times in our lives. To help someone to feel good about who they are as a result of the love we give is sometimes even more rewarding than the love we receive ourselves. When we can let love flow out of us as much as we let love flow into us, we grow. Before my cancer, I was a person who found it extremely difficult to show and accept love, and this inability to show love contributed greatly to the break down of my relationship with my son's father. It took cancer for me to learn how to let others love me and to realise that in order to love and be loved, I needed to open up and allow myself to be vulnerable. I learned that vulnerability can be a strength rather than a weakness. When I finally learned that the love I gave and the love I allowed myself to receive were of equal importance, many things in my heart began to heal. This lesson allowed me to open myself to let the love and care of others flow into my life so that I could be cared for and nurtured as I needed to be.

We Are Connected By Love

As I went through chemotherapy, I sought help and support from an excellent charity called The Haven, which runs a number of centres in London, Hereford, and Leeds. The Haven offers free support, information, and complementary therapies to anyone affected emotionally by breast cancer and the associated treatments.

Their free services cover a wide range of emotional, physical and, practical support, which includes over forty complimentary services. I was seen by an amazing therapist to whom I poured my heart out. She listened, encouraged, and supported me while I unburdened myself. She then set about helping me to arrive at a place where I could heal myself emotionally and come to terms with everything that had happened.

My therapy sessions left me feeling as though I had breathed a sigh of relief. In them I was able to take off the brave and stoic face I had forced myself to wear for so long, especially during my illness. It was reassuring to be able to express my true feelings without worrying that my thoughts were burdening someone else and without worrying about being judged for the honesty in the thoughts I shared. In one session, I broke down into tears because of the huge relief that came when I admitted I couldn't make it through my treatment alone and that I needed someone to hold me, hug me, say that they would be there for me, and share some of the burden of what I was going through.

At one point, my therapist told me that we are all connected. I went home after that session and started to think more about what she said. I have to admit, I was skeptical. I wondered how we could possibly be connected when I personally felt so abandoned by my ex, and so lost. If we were truly all connected, shouldn't I feel a little less alone?

As the days wore on and I continued to think about it, I slowly began to embrace the truth of her words. At one point, I felt very strongly that she was right and that, yes, we really are all connected. This became even clearer to me as I welcomed guests into my home and as my son and I interacted more and more with them. They began to have an impact on our daily lives, and for the short time they were with us, I watched as our lives became more intertwined with theirs. My son and I began to rely on them for companionship and, in a strange way, support, which came in the form of a diversion from my illness. They played with Nicholas, giving him the attention I wasn't always in a mental or physical state to give him. There were times when they would watch over him while I would take a bit of time to rest.

One of the French girls by the name of Priscilla would take him to and from the nursery. Christina, who was with us for eight weeks, left us and found her own flat in London, but she would still visit us on the weekends and regularly take Nicholas to the park. Marilyn, a retiree from Phoenix, Arizona, who stayed with us for four months over a summer, gave us one of the best summers I can remember. Marilyn is one of the most loving and giving people I have ever known, and she immediately became part of the family. She accompanied us on weekends to my sister's house and she celebrated Easter and the fourth of July with us. We even visited London together. Marilyn made such a tremendous impression on Nicholas that he even began to see her as a surrogate grandmother.

A wonderful couple, Élio and Silvia from Portugal, stayed with us during the first Christmas after my mastectomy. I'll linger on this story for a moment because it is one of the most beautiful experiences I've had in my life. I had my mastectomy in October of 2012. I remember feeling relieved to be finished with the procedure, exhausted from it, grateful to have it behind me, and extremely lonely, especially because Christmas was just around the corner. Though it was still a few months away, people around me were already making plans to celebrate the holidays. I had been through so much upheaval with my cancer and treatment that it felt strange to plan for the holidays as usual, as if nothing had happened. So, when my family asked what I would do for Christmas and where I would be celebrating the holiday, I remember feeling as if all I wanted to do was to take some time to care for my son and myself over the festive season. More than that, I desperately wanted a Christmas where *I* was cared for, but I was too proud to ask. And I didn't even feel as though I should have had to ask.

Somehow, I managed to convince myself that I would have an amazing Christmas, even if I wasn't completely sure how. I declared in my own heart that this Christmas would be a very special one for my son, because we deserved it. I made it quite clear to my family that, although I didn't have any specific plans, this Christmas was going to be amazing.

I ended up inviting two of my oldest friends to join us for the festivities, even though I still didn't have a clue about the details. However, fate had its own plans for us. The night before Christmas Eve, I received a booking request for a room in my home from a man and his wife from Portugal. They wanted a room for ten days over the Christmas holiday. In the booking request, the man explained to me that he had a booking elsewhere that had been cancelled at the last minute. He had seen the photos of my home and read the reviews and he and his wife wanted to be my guests. Through the words in his email, I could sense his nervousness and felt he needed reassuring. Even though I had been through so much with my health, I received his request with gratitude for the extra money the booking would bring my way. So, I picked up the phone and called him in Portugal. Initially, he was taken aback that a person such as myself that he didn't even know would call him. But then the conversation relaxed, and he came across in such a warm and friendly way that we hit it off quite well.

The couple arrived just past midnight on Christmas Eve and I welcomed them inside with a warm hug and a cup of tea. Instead of letting them drink alone in their room, I invited them to have a drink with me. From that moment on, we got on like a house on fire. Élio, the gentleman, insisted on cooking Christmas dinner, which was a mixture of Portuguese and English cuisine and lots and lots of wine. They went on to look after Nicholas and me with love and care. Even after spending their days sightseeing in London, they would return home to cook wonderful, multi-course meals for us in the evening. The good company, love, care, and diversion from my woes that Élio and his wife Sylvia brought into my home made me feel so warmed, so nurtured, so cared for, and so blessed. Our Christmas that year was truly amazing, just as I had determined it would be. To think that two complete strangers could come into my life to show us so much love, compassion, and consideration is incredibly humbling. It was a beautiful lesson in realising that love is indeed all around.

After the holidays were over, my sister called and enquired as to whether our holidays had been as "amazing" as I said they would be. Of course, I had to reply that, yes, it had turned out to be amazing and beautiful because I had requested that it be amazing, because I had believed it would be, and because I was open to receive the gift of companionship and care from complete strangers.

The year following their departure, I decided to start a blog about my experience with cancer. After reading my blog, Élio and Sylvia invited me and Nicholas to holiday with them at their home in Benavente, Portugal, where they again took complete care of us for a week. I am filled with gratitude for these two, who have become great friends and who have been such a gift to me.

Another person from whom I received love and support is my neighbour Suzanne, who I had previously only exchanged pleasantries with before my cancer diagnosis. She was instrumental in encouraging me to go to my doctor to have my lump checked out initially, but after the diagnosis, she became a source of love and care. She researched the best qualified surgeon in my area to perform the mastectomy, she researched another plastic surgeon to perform the breast reconstruction, and she harangued the hospital to arrange transport to take me to and from the hospital and much more. She became my friend and champion.

These are just a few examples of the amazing people I have had the good fortune of letting into my life. I bless and thank each one of them for the love and kindness they have shown to my son and me during our time of greatest need.

Though I was grateful for each act of kindness received from so many people in my life, there was a degree of being overwhelmed by it as well, to the extent that I don't think I could really appreciate fully at the time just how lucky and blessed I was. In a way, I was carried away on a wave of kindness and the pace was so fast that I wasn't able to pause to deeply appreciate so much kindness. Now, almost three years later, I look back and am amazed by the depth of kindness shown to me by the people who helped me. I am beyond grateful to God for bringing these people into my life and blessing me with an open mind and an open heart to receive so much love from so many directions.

These acts of kindness towards me and my son made me realise that, yes, we are all connected. What we do has an impact on someone else and on someone else after that. It's almost as though there is a rippling effect and that ripple can go either way. When we're unkind to someone, that unkindness affects how that person interacts with the next person they encounter. If we are kind to someone, they in turn will share that kindness with someone else, who will then share it with someone else, and so on. That ripple gains momentum and a life of its own, spreading in ever-increasing circles.

It's quite striking when you realise that you have the power to impact another's life in such a profound way. I remember when I was receiving chemotherapy in the hospital for my cancer and I thought it remarkable that all around me were people receiving chemotherapy. Each one of us was connected to the others through our emotions, thoughts, desires, aspirations, fears, hopes, and also by our love. In that chemotherapy room, there was so much love and fear, and I was part of those who felt it, and they were part of me, too.

Now, when dealing with people, I always try to deal with them in such a way that they are encouraged to feel our connection and that they feel appreciated and worthy. In so doing, they will in turn want to perpetuate those positive and soul-enriching feelings to others they meet, and our connection with others will grow. Today, as a result of the realisation of connectedness I gained through therapy, I have let go of the negative feelings and negative energy I felt related to so many things, but especially towards Nicholas' father. All I feel now is a deep gratitude and appreciation for how fortunate I was to meet him and how generous he was to have given our son to me. I bless him and send him love and eternal gratitude for his kindness of spirit, and I wish him every happiness.

Connectedness is Bigger than Ourselves

The biggest demonstration of connectedness in my life came via the love and support I received from people I had never met before. Through the hands and hearts of strangers, I felt pulled and tugged by the cord of our invisible connection.

I went to receive my first round of chemotherapy with a friend of mine who took the day off work to accompany me to the hospital. When we arrived, the ward was chaotic. There was only one nurse on duty when there should have been two, and she was solely responsible for administering the correct dosage of the chemotherapy drugs to at least half a dozen patients. I was very concerned about having the treatment, and seeing the situation in the ward filled me with even more trepidation.

I turned around to my friend and mimed to her that I wanted to leave, which we did. The following day we returned. I was determined to have the treatment and thankfully there were the required number of nurses on duty. This was good news as far as I was concerned; however, I was still quite fearful and that fear was written all over my face. An elderly man sat waiting to have his dosage of the drug. He was alone. We sat next to him on the sofa waiting to be called to the ward. He could see the fear on my face and, turning to me, he put his hand on my arm and with a very kind and reassuring smile on his face said, "Don't worry. I've been coming here on and off for the past two years and it's not half as bad as you think; you'll be fine." I can't tell you how reassured I felt after he said those words; his kindness had touched me.

Due to the side effects of the chemotherapy I was finding it extremely difficult to summon the energy to look after my son. With the aim of securing some help at home, I got in touch with a local charity called Sure Start that was able to send a volunteer once a week for a few hours to help me care for him. We would have tea or coffee and chat, or we would go shopping, and she would spend time with Nicholas, and I found myself looking forward so much to Fridays. Just having somebody for two hours that was focussed on me and my son made a tremendous difference for me. I felt I could relax and connect with the lady from the charity, which proved to be a great distraction.

When I consider the difference a complete stranger made in my life by showing me that love between humans can transcend so many differences, I started to consider what an absolutely wonderful world it would be if we remembered that we are constantly making these differences. I've realised that whatever happens to another person affects me too, because I am connected to each person I encounter in my life. I began to embrace my responsibility to each person I interacted with, recognising that the way I treated them and the love I shared would have an impact on the lives they touched as well, and so on and so on. To see our lives from such a perspective is so beautiful, so powerful, and so transformational.

Truly, the only regret I have is that it took so long into my adult life for me to learn that the only way to experience wonderful demonstrations of love is by first being open to giving and receiving them. When we shut ourselves off from either side of that equation, the love that is all around cannot make its way into our lives. Like so many things I have learned through my interaction with cancer, I always hope that my experiences will help others see the truths I've discovered *without* a horrible disease such as cancer having to be the demanding teacher. Part of our connectedness includes me connecting with you and sharing the lessons my journey has taught, because they simply don't belong to me; they belong to all of us.

Chapter 6

EXPRESSION OF GRATITUDE

"Cultivate the habit of being grateful for every good thing that comes to you, and to give thanks continuously. And because all things have contributed to your advancement, you should include all things in your gratitude."
[Ralph Waldo Emerson]

W e often hear that gratitude is important for happiness, and that we should be grateful. We even prompt children to express gratitude when they're given something. Most religious practices and philosophies contain a component of gratitude in their tenets. It's not a novel concept, and yet, when you meet a person or have a friend or family member who has *discovered the power of gratitude for themselves*, you would think they felt as though they had just discovered gravity. Honestly, this is how the experience of learning to express gratitude has felt to me as well.

It's not that I was an ungrateful person before my cancer. I said thank you, and I appreciated things I was given and the opportunities I had to learn and earn and grow. However, through my cancer battle, I can definitely say that gratitude has taken a new place of importance in my life.

What Is Gratitude?

To me, gratitude is appreciating what we have in the here and now. It's actually stopping to say thank you to God and to the universe; it is being thankful for all things, good and bad. It's not only *feeling* that we are glad to have what we have, but it is *expressing* that feeling. I do believe gratitude wells up in many people's hearts without it ever being expressed, either for lack of words to express their thanks or for fear of demonstrating weakness by showing an emotion. A very important aspect of gratitude is expression.

Why? Well, I have come to believe that gratitude begets gratitude. In other words, the more grateful we are, and the more frequently we express this gratitude, the more reason we will have to be grateful and the more experiences we will have that trigger gratitude. It's a cycle. And it's a cycle that can change your life.

After I was diagnosed with cancer, I felt almost strange that I suddenly started to see all the small reasons why I should be grateful. I even began seeing reason to be grateful for my cancer and for its timing. I realised how grateful I was that I was diagnosed with breast cancer a year after my son was born, not a year before. Had I been diagnosed a year before, I probably never would have had my son. It is thought that the hormone injections necessary with IVF to stimulate the ovaries could possibly have an effect on the cells that cause breast cancer, so there is a real possibility that had I been diagnosed sooner, no doctor would proceeded with treating me with IVF.

I also began to be grateful that I didn't have a job at the time of my diagnosis. I had no real means, no income, but instead of resenting that, I'm grateful for it. It meant I didn't have to worry about disappointing an employer with the time I needed to care for my health and, more importantly, it meant I found myself in a position where I needed to take in guests. As I've already mentioned, taking paying guests into my home in order to pay my bills has been a tremendous blessing in so many ways. Truly, not having a job led me to a way to provide for myself and my son that has played an incredible part in my overcoming breast cancer and my growth as an individual.

I began to see so many things for which to be thankful. I was fortunate enough to give birth to my son before cancer declared itself. My cancer was found early enough to be able to deal with it effectively. The type of breast cancer I had has a very high treatment success rate and the treatment options are advanced. I was of an age where I could still enjoy my son, despite the treatment. I had family and friends and, in some cases, total strangers rally round to show me love and support. I was able to keep my diagnosis from my elderly mum who perhaps would not have been able to cope with my illness. Through the help of friends, I was able to identify a top surgeon experienced in mastectomies, and I received first-class, free care. I could have had breast reconstruction on both breasts too, which would have all been free. I was grateful cancer treatment has come such a long way and that I could call on the support of charities like Macmillan Cancer Support, The Haven, and Sure Start Services. I was grateful that my faith in God allowed me to be ever hopeful that He would bring me through my illness as a stronger person. I was grateful for all the love and support that surrounded me, which humbled me immensely.

All of these things were reasons to be grateful, but of all the things I am grateful for, I am most grateful that I never lost hope. I was reminded always to focus on the positive and on all the things I appreciate in my life. In so doing, I found even more things to be grateful for, such as a child's smile that reminded me of my son, my walks through the park each morning to take my son to nursery, being able to look at the sky, breathing fresh air, and feeling lucky to be alive. All of these little things were really big things. They were little reasons to feel major gratitude and to continue being positive and hopeful.

Express Gratitude Daily

We should express gratitude daily. I keep a gratitude journal and every day I write the things I am grateful for, both big and small. Nothing is too small to be grateful for. For example, somebody gave me his seat on the bus, and I came home and wrote a thank you for that. All kinds of things go into my gratitude book. *Thank you for a beautiful day, thank you for the sun shining, and the birds singing. Thank you for good health, thank you for having friends and family around.* These are seemingly small things, but expressing gratitude for them makes them big things. Expressing your gratitude for a small thing is like picking up a pebble, being grateful for it, and watching it turn into a gem that you treasure and cherish.

The more I express gratitude in my gratitude journal, the more things I find myself being grateful for. It energises me and gives me a feeling of being supported. It helps me stay grounded, and to an extent, it puts my life into perspective. This way I focus on the important things in life and don't become so engrossed and worked up over silly things, which can so easily distract us from our greater aspirations.

To anyone who will listen, I like to encourage others to take some time out of each and every day to express gratitude. Whether it's early in the morning or the last thing you do at night, schedule some time every day to notice, recognise, and be grateful for those little things in your life. By pulling the reasons out of your heart and onto the page, you are not just feeling gratitude, you are expressing it. In addition, express gratitude to others as well. Send a thank you card to somebody for being nice or to someone who took the time to help you or talk to you on the phone. Call, send a card, and thank them for their assistance. This has such an impact on the person receiving your expression of gratitude; you may never even know how much it affected their day positively. But it also affects you. Expressing gratitude always increases your gratitude.

The Advantages of Expressing Gratitude

I have found that expressing gratitude makes me a happier, more appreciative person, who is more tuned into life and the lives of those around me. I guess you could say that it has helped me realise that life is not all about me.

When I worked in the corporate world, I was consumed by my ambition and determination to achieve goals and make as much money as possible. Seldom did I take any time out of my day to say thank you or to appreciate my situation or express appreciation to and for my colleagues, my clients, and my family. I think I must have been under the illusion that it is your achievements in life that determine the type of person you are. In other words, if you're successful, it is because you deserve it and have earned it. Since being diagnosed with cancer, this belief has been turned on its head. Now, I am grateful for every day that I am still here. I am grateful to know that I have learned to slow down, lose my nonsensical pursuit of achievement and self-importance, and simply be grateful to be me. I no longer pretend to be a high-flying recruitment consultant who is so fantastic at finding people jobs, as proven by my bank balance. Rather, I am just myself, and I am grateful to be alive and able to help others, in business and in life.

There are other advantages to expressing gratitude. Surprisingly, many of them are not interpersonal or related to our outlook of the world. Rather, there is a growing body of scientific evidence that indicates gratitude has physical and psychological advantages as well. Physically, expressing gratitude improves the functioning of our immune systems, helps achieve and maintain a healthy blood pressure, decreases the occurrences of pains and aches, makes us more motivated to exercise and pursue a healthy lifestyle, and it helps us sleep more soundly.

Psychologically, expressing gratitude helps us feel more alert and awake, both physically and intuitively. We experience higher levels of joy, pleasure, and optimism, among other positive emotions. And, gratitude is infectious. Just try living around a grateful person without feeling uplifted and grateful yourself. For all of these reasons, I truly believe that the expression of gratitude is the way forward, for all of us, to improve our own life and the lives of those around us. There are often difficult situations around us, and we want to help others, but we don't always know how. A simple word to someone in a tight spot about your own experience expressing gratitude, as well as expressing gratitude for that person, can work wonders.

Gratitude is a Choice

As mentioned in the quote at the beginning of this chapter, we should learn to be grateful for all aspects of our life, not only the good. Being only thankful for positive things is a trap many fall into. I certainly needed to learn this lesson. Often when something tragic or frustrating or disappointing occurs, our gratitude flies out the window.

It is easier to have a *feeling* of gratitude when things are going well. But what many don't realize and what I learned is that gratitude goes beyond a feeling—it is actually a choice. When things aren't going our way, the feeling of gratitude not only feels elusive, but non-existent. It's hard to feel grateful when you learn you have cancer, when you grow weary of searching for your soul mate, when you have difficulty conceiving the child you so desperately want, or any number of experiences we go through in life. And yet, it is in these times and through these crises that we have the most to gain by *choosing* to express gratitude.

When we discover the power of seeing the world around us, the good and the bad, and practicing to choose gratitude every step of the way, we will finally arrive at this beautiful conclusion: gratitude has the ability to energise when we are feeling low; it has the power to heal our brokenness; it is able to bring hope in times of despair; and it helps us cope when sad, troubling and trying circumstances surround us.

A Challenge

My challenge to you is this: begin today to look for reasons to be grateful and express your gratitude however you can, which can be in a journal, directly to people, audibly to yourself, or in whatever way you come up with. More importantly, challenge yourself to truly feel gratitude and choose gratitude for every single thing in your life, including the wonderful things as well as the trying things. Your existence will be uplifted, your happiness and joy will be made abundant and full, and you will be amazed by the difference this choice makes in your life.

As I have said so many times in this book, I sincerely hope that nothing as horrible as cancer will ever be the catalyst that nudges you towards discovering many of the truths I've shared. It doesn't need to be that way. For myself, I am so blessed and beyond grateful for the fact that through my personal catalyst, cancer, I have had the opportunity to discover the joy of choosing gratitude. To have learned this lesson for myself and to have had the opportunity to share this lesson with you, has made it all so very worthwhile.

Chapter 7

STEPPING INTO THE LIGHT

"Though my soul may set in darkness,
it will rise in perfect light;
I have loved the stars too fondly
to be fearful of the night."
[Sarah Williams]

T here is an old Chinese proverb that says, "When the student is ready, the teacher will appear." This is really quite appropriate for the experiences that I have shared throughout this book. My illness brought me to a place where I was a ready student, and the teacher most definitely appeared. To me, this is the essence of stepping into the light. We are all students and we each have different lessons to learn, but we have this in common: we can choose to step into the light and present ourselves for the lessons of our teacher, or we can stay hidden in the shadows until we are dragged into the light, ready or not.

Stepping into the light need not be scary. There are too many wonderful experiences to find when we step forward and present ourselves, all of which enrich us and blossom our lives into something beautiful. I look back on my life and who I was before cancer, and I honestly don't know whether I ever would have stepped into the light on my own, or if having cancer was always going to be the necessary instigator to drag me into a place where I could be taught so many important lessons. Either way, I have learned much the last few years, all of which I am grateful for. My illness has caused me to move forward in celebrating my disasters while giving me so much to be grateful for. Without breast cancer, I would not have the happy, fulfilled life that I have today. Without breast cancer, I would not have been able to write this book, which has filled me with tremendous joy. Without writing this book, I would have been unable to share my experiences with other breast cancer survivors and those battling other hardships.

Cancer truly has saved my life. Today, I am able to see two sides of the same coin—joy and pain, sadness and despair. Elation and happiness are on the other side of every difficult challenge and disastrous situation we face. Whenever we meet one side of the coin, there is always another side that we must stretch to see in order to gain hope, joy, and opportunities for self-growth. Cancer showed me the other side of the coin—the beautiful and blessed side, the side that has made me a stronger and better person.

By stepping into the light, I found the other side of the coin.

Faith is Strength

My faith, a gift from my mum, gave me the strength and ability to cope with my fears. I feared not having enough, not being enough, not surviving, not being a good mum, and not having a full and beautiful life. Although I couldn't make fear go away, I learned to no longer be paralysed by it. I had to learn how not to give in to fear.

Faith was my stepping stone. The benefit of this is I now feel I can achieve so much more than ever before. *I can* have the life I want. Although fear will always be there in some form, my faith keeps me from being governed by it.

Particularly related to breast cancer, I never thought I would have been one of those "1 in 8 women" who is diagnosed with breast cancer. However, when it happened to me, my faith supported me through it. You do not have to be of any particular faith to cling to the deep and saving knowledge that there is a higher power that is always ready to assist us if we are open to it. The simple requirement is belief that there is a something outside of yourself. I refer to him as God because I believe in God, but there are other religions and deities that people have faith in too. The main thing is to lean wholeheartedly on the fact that there is something out there who is bigger than you that can bear your fears and doubts and carry you past them. And through cancer, I've seen my faith grow.

My faith has manifested itself in many ways. I remember one particular incident when I was in a supermarket and felt an overwhelming feeling of happiness and gratitude, just a few days after I was diagnosed with cancer. I couldn't understand why I felt this way when circumstances at the time were so dire. But I was uplifted and carried forward by an overwhelming sense that everything was going to be alright. I smiled a big smile and a gentleman in the aisle looked at me and said, "Wow, what a lovely smile!" I remember thinking, *What do I have to smile about?* It was my faith smiling, I'm sure of it. Something stronger than me was carrying me and lifting my burden.

It is Never Too Late to Change your Life

We all find ourselves in situations that are so desperate and difficult that we think, *It's too late; there's nothing I can do now to change this.* I'm here to tell you that my experiences have taught me it is never too late; you are never too old to change your life. All you have to do is want to change and set a goal for yourself. Once you know what you *do* want, or at least what you *don't* want, reach out for it and have faith. Whether your faith is in God, the Universe, or any deity or spiritual power outside of yourself, it doesn't matter so long as you have faith that it's never too late. No matter how desperate, sad, difficult, or crazy your life might seem, if you are prepared to take responsibility and to have faith, you also have the ability to change. The ability is within you. We can all access the strength within to change and take responsibility for our lives. We can have the life we dream of having.

Being Open Keeps Us Connected

Every time I prayed or meditated during my dealings with cancer, there was always a consistent message I received: to be open. There was always a large part of me that remained closed to others. It may have been a vulnerability issue, but thankfully I've learned that we must stay open to others and that being open does not mean being weak. Openness does not negate your power or your authority, and it does not make you a victim. Once you realise that by opening yourself to others place you in a position to receive all of the support, good wishes, and good intentions of beautiful and amazing people, you may wonder why you ever closed yourself off in the first place.

When something difficult happens in life, resist the urge to withdraw and shut out the world. It is better to turn outwards and tap into the love of those surrounding you.

This is not just for your survival and strength; it's actually for others as well. Relying on our connections with others makes those we rely on feel good and gives them a sense of being helpful and having purpose, thereby strengthening their self-worth. It gives you strength, courage, and support to know that you're not alone. There are lots of people out there to support you, love you and care for you. Setting aside my inclination to stay closed off from others led me down a path towards recognising and benefitting from all the love and care that exists when we are open to connectedness with others. In fact, I would not have survived without it.

Today, I am at peace with myself and with life. Though I don't have the disposable income I once had, I make ends meet. My house, out of financial necessity and also by choice is full of guests who enrich my life. I am much happier today than I was when I was employed full time. I can now appreciate the simple things in life, like the fact that I have a family, I have very good friends, and I have guests with whom I share meals and a glass of wine or a cup of tea. I can actually sit down at the kitchen table and talk to my guests and get to know them, find out their story, and feel connected to people from all walks of life.

I am now able to look outside of myself and have great peace in knowing that my life is no longer about how much money I earn. My priorities have changed so much for the better. I've gone from being stressed out to being a mum who spends every day with her son, a mum who is her own boss and manages her own time in a way that saves time for family and friends. I find time to help my guests and give to others more than I ever hope to receive from them.

I still feel fear, for any number of reasons, but my life is no longer governed by it. My fear of shortage has gone away. Having faced what I faced and come through it a better, stronger, and more compassionate person, I now have the courage and strength to pursue the life that I want. And what do I want in my life? I want opportunities to share how cancer saved my life. I want to help people develop a mindset that will equip them to meet life's challenges, find the peace they want, and appreciate the here and now. I want to help others experience our connectedness for themselves and to be open to it.

Today my life is very different than it was two years ago. I feel that I can conquer the world. This is not a statement born of arrogance or conceit, but born of faith, self-confidence, and humility. My faith has grown tremendously as a result of the experiences of life in general and as a result of my cancer, in particular. I am filled with humility, because I feel as though I have been given a second chance at life. This time, I am living a better, more fulfilled, more connected life with a purpose and meaning greater than myself. In truth, cancer not only saved my life, it restarted my life. My life, with meaning and purpose, started when I was diagnosed with cancer. Cancer was my beginning, not my ending. I have stepped into the light, and my life can only get better.

Chapter 8

A PRAYER

M y prayer for each of you, is embodied in the words of this poem. Our lives are short, yet full of so many opportunities to let go of fear and doubt and give in to the amazing journey of loving ourselves and each other. May your days be blessed.

You carry the cure within you.
Everything that comes your way is blessed.
The Creator gives you one more day.
Stand on the neck of Fearful Mind.

Do not wait to open your heart.

Let yourself go into the Mystery.
Sometimes the threads have no weave.
The price of not loving yourself is high.

Jim Cohn

ACKNOWLEDGEMENTS

A big thank you to my editor Monica LaSarre, without whom this dream to write this book would never have been fulfilled. Thank you to Gosia Gorna, my therapist. Without her encouragement and support, I never would have started this project. To Tiffany Missiha, my coach, who gave me the confidence and self-belief I needed to make myself vulnerable in order to share my story with others. I am grateful also to Margaret Barclay, my kinesiologist, and Hazel Du Preez, my dietician, whose treatment made all the difference to my recovery. To the surgeon and staff at King George and Queen's Hospital, you will forever have my gratitude for the excellent medical care I received during my illness. To the Consultant Plastic and Reconstructive Surgeon, at the Royal London Hospital, Miss Hasu Patel and her team, thank you for your skill and expertise in reconstructing my breasts. You and your team have done an amazing job. I will always be tremendously grateful to my neighbour Suzanne Selby, who was like a guardian angel to me, providing invaluable support at the time of my greatest need. To Élio Oliveira and Sylvia Mateus, who for ten days looked after Nicholas and me, making sure that we had a wonderful Christmas. To my sister Veronica and my brother John and all the rest of my family and friends who were always there for Nicholas and me showering us with love and support throughout. To my dear friends Anne Gue, Maureen Clyne, and Violet DeMowbray, thank you for travelling with me to Rome and Portugal at a moment's notice. Yvonne having you present at my chemotherapy session made all the difference, thank you. Marilyn Newman, thank you for your friendship, help and support. The love and kindness you showed us impacted greatly on our lives. To all the guests who have stayed at my home and showed us love and support, thank you. I would like to say a special thank you to my mum whom I love dearly and for whom I have tremendous admiration. She is my hero, who taught me that everything is possible when you have faith in God.

Photograph by Magnús Andersen

Book cover by Tania Cearreta

EPILOGUE

I am happy that I wrote this book. It was important to me at the time of writing that others could benefit from it. We all have trauma in our lives and I really hope that the book can help others. Despite the challenges I faced while writing this book, I was determined to explore my own vulnerability and re-visit experiences in my life I would rather forget.

We all want to feel good about ourselves and reach our goals in life. In order to achieve this in my opinion, it is important for us to take away something positive from life's challenges and use this as a rudder to steer us to the life we want.

I have been cancer free for almost three years and it is only now I have come to realize that everyone and every event in my life has played a part in shaping who I am, how I relate to others and my view on the world in general. My journey through life thus far, and my encounter with cancer has helped me to see and appreciate the important things in life: love, family and friends. It has helped me to appreciate the simple beauty of life itself. This in my opinion, is when cancer saved my life.

ABOUT THE AUTHOR

M illicent is a mum, an entrepreneur, a cancer survivor, fundraiser and an author. She has been cancer free for almost 3 years and, testament to the advice in her book, has rerouted the skills she developed from recruitment into a new business as a motivational coach, helping people to explore different mind sets and develop a positive view on life and challenges.

She is fundraising for The Haven Breast Cancer Support in the UK and she is waiting to start with Macmillan Cancer Support to go into schools and colleges and talk to people about her experience of having cancer and how she coped.

Printed in Great Britain
by Amazon.co.uk, Ltd.,
Marston Gate.